The Folding of the Wings

poems by

Frank William Finney

Finishing Line Press
Georgetown, Kentucky

The Folding of the Wings

Copyright © 2022 by Frank William Finney
ISBN 978-1-64662-953-4 First Edition
All rights reserved under International and Pan-American Copyright Conventions. No part of this book may be reproduced in any manner whatsoever without written permission from the publisher, except in the case of brief quotations embodied in critical articles and reviews.

ACKNOWLEDGMENTS

CatheXis Northwest Press: The Passing of Poodles
Millennial Pulp Literary Magazine: Winter: A Flashback
Poetry Pacific: The Lighthouse Keepers
Poor Yorick: The Poet's Mask Issue: The Flight From Bangkok
A Portrait of New England: The Earl of Nostalgia; Horseshoes
The Raw Art Review: Haunted House
Red River Review: Prufrock's Teddy Bear
Rue Scribe: Elegy For Ernie
The Showbear Family Circus: Hitchhiking in the '70s
Slipstream Magazine: The Night Nurse
Streetlight Magazine: The Pines; Finish Line
Terror House Magazine: A Limo at Last
Unstamatic: Celebrity's Will
Vine Leaves Literary Journal: Night Shuts In; Happy Hour at the Monet Café; A Cold Eye
Tales from the Changeover: Workers Write!: As I Left the Office for the Last Time

Publisher: Leah Huete de Maines
Editor: Christen Kincaid
Cover Art and Design: Trevor Finney, Instagram- @TREVFINNA
Author Photo: Trevor Finney

Order online: www.finishinglinepress.com
also available on amazon.com

Author inquiries and mail orders:
Finishing Line Press
PO Box 1626
Georgetown, Kentucky 40324
USA

Table of Contents

The Lighthouse Keepers 1

Prufrock's Teddy Bear 2

A Cold Eye 3

Happy Hour at the Monet Café 4

Hitchhiking in the '70s 5

The Earl of Nostalgia 6

The Passing of Poodles 7

Celebrity's Will 8

The Pines 9

Haunted House 10

As I Left the Office for the Last Time 11

Winter: A Flashback 12

Horseshoes 13

Elegy for Ernie 14

A Limo at Last 15

Game of Clones 16

Departure 17

The Flight from Bangkok 18

Finish Line 19

Night Shuts In 20

For my mother, in memory of my father

*Let the flight through the sky end in the folding
of the wings over the nest.*
—Rabindranath Tagore

The Lighthouse Keepers

Puppeteers buckling sandals
at the top of the steps.

By day they chase shadows
of sail and scull.

By night and storm
do drowned men speak
to trespassless towers
the silence of seaweed?

Prufrock's Teddy Bear

After Alfie died
They stuffed me in a shoebox with
The tie clips, the cufflinks, and all those combs he kept
For all those years, for reasons never made clear to me.
A few relatives came and went through everything.
A cousin made off with his coffee spoons; a nephew
Took his toaster and tea cups; some lonely-looking woman,
Her hair in a bun, carried away his autographed copy of
Cakes and Ale.

And indeed his same kin found it worthwhile, after all,
To settle me here—underpriced and underrated—a relic of
Some obscene suburban jumble sale,

To perch me upon a top hat between his pipe collection
And the rag the moths made of his morning coat.

To add me to the realm of 'trams and dusty trees'.
This is NOT, I presume, where he'd wish me to be.

Privy, as I was, to his deepest secrets—
The women, and the mermaids—I heard it all.

Confused, though, he was, from time to time . . .
I still like to think I understood him.

Oh, let us dispense with a tedious argument:
Lest you lot forget: we shared the same bed.

A Cold Eye

As I pass the place
where he crashed his jeep,

the fates burn the broom
of Monday's witch.

As sirens sing behind the pines,
crumbs swim circles in the wine.

Out like a drunk
on a flagstone floor

your neck's on the rail
and the train's on time.

Happy Hour at the Monet Café

'Yes, but you make me think',
he said, passing her a pickled onion.

'Yes, and you make me laugh', she said,
fishing the mint from a spent mojito.

Meanwhile, the barman divided a lemon.
Outside the rain blurred a passing bus.

Hitchhiking in the 70's

Impossible impasse:
your guitar case kicks at knee level,
one thumb in the air. Both eyes marooned
on the taillights ahead.

The callous cold. The gloves too thin.
Red numb thumbs exposed to a curse
the woods shouts out to everyone
who walks near here this time of year.

There must be ice in a person's life.
No, I hear a waterfall. An irregular heart
beat even the trees can sense

when a driver in a pickup
slows down, takes a look and
then speeds off
as if she's seen the future.

The Earl of Nostalgia
(for E.D. Clark)

On those Saturday nights
late summers and early falls—

we drummed on the dashboard
of his '65 Mustang

to every Beatle song we knew
till the beer was gone and the

daylight found us
on High Street Hill with

bags under our eyes
singing Good Day Sunshine.

The Passing of Poodles
(quatre vignettes pour les caniches)

1.
Nanette: hit on a holiday
by a cowboy in a Mack who cursed his luck
before driving away.

2.
Monique: mowed down in the middle
of Old Great Road by a woman in a wagon
wearing socks that glowed.

3.
Charee: my favorite, lived the longest
of the three till she was struck down
with epilepsy.

4.
Three dogs take turns now, walking me,
when I visit their bones
at the pet cemetery.

Celebrity's Will

Send my brothers the rest of my suits;
My sister, the towels and whatever
surviving pets she might like.

Divide the children
among the houses and land.

When the ashes are ready,
throw them off the Golden Gate.

For years and years,
I dreamt I jumped.

Better late than never.

The Pines

Behind Snow Drive,
rusty needles led to a pine grove,
where we made little circles
with dirty rocks
and lit little fires
with matches lifted
from the corner store.
These days the pines
that survive make little circles
of shade in a trail
of three-car garages
and realtors' signs.
The old store stays open
in our heads.

Haunted House

On Saturdays, my father treated us
to a model kit
from the hobby shelves of the
local store.

My brothers always went for cars
or planes.
I went for the monsters,
This time, Frankenstein's—

its body parts formed of
plastic and glue—
the whole deal shrouded in
glossy enamel.

This time my choice
came back to haunt me.

Unable to endure the aspect
of the being . . .
unable to compose my mind to sleep

My howling spooked every room
in the house
and my mother's grumbling
chased Dad and the monster
down the long, dark hall.

Strangers still hear
the echoes.

As I Left the Office for the Last Time

The books
on the shelves

might as well
have been blank.

A career's worth
of scribblings

as needless now
as the keys I tossed

in the mail bin
as the door clicked

its tongue
behind me.

Winter: A Flashback

We chugged can after can
of half-frozen beer
and waited under a streetlight
for the blizzard they promised
on the six o'clock news.

Once in while a car slid by.
A cop in a cruiser crossed
the turnpike bridge.

Half a mile down the road
in a box on the hill,
my father's widow crossed
herself thrice when the clock
struck one and the snowstorm whirled
the world around.

Horseshoes
  (Livermore, Maine)

There was something sacred
about their Sunday ritual:
The solemn march from the bench
to the pitching box.

The communion of steel mouths
clanging like bells beneath the
stained-glass sky.

We stood in our pajamas
at the kitchen window
as the flashes flung towards heaven
came down with a thud—

Dark clouds of dust
across the old dirt road.

Elegy for Ernie
    (In Memory of Ernie Minichiello)

First time among friends
I didn't hear you laugh.

All I could hear
were the engines outside

humming a dirge
at the traffic lights.

A Limo at Last

Faces in the windows
on both sides of the street

can vouch for the manners
of the young chauffeur

as he led the old couple
to a pristine limousine

as the gossip floundered
from house to house.

They say the couple
had a son

who was ostracized
for playing ostrich

in the vestry
with the altar boys.

They say he smoked up
a warehouse worth

of cigarettes
in sun, snow, or rain

before he finally disappeared
in a *closed confessional*

some few days before the limo pulled up
near the old couple's lawn

where he used to smoke and stare
from house to house.

Game of Clones

We sit down
to play Monopoly.

You stand up
to count your cash.

I roll the dice
and end up bankrupt.

You fold up the board
and walk away.

Departure

I arrived at the counter
in a fog

And then my bags
moved on the belt . . .

Soon I saw the tiny lights.
And then, of course, the clouds.

The Flight from Bangkok

I had no urge to watch a movie. Even the music held no appeal.
The nurse in my head said: drink, man, drink—
but nevertheless, beware the loo ...

When the mask came off to face the food, I couldn't find
my appetite. When the hostie returned to pick up the tray,
I tried my best to smile back with my eyes.

Finish Line

The knees will need braces.
The bones rebel.
The memory
turn traitor: rust to dust.
Hoops and hurdles.
Heartbreak Hills.
Fast as a mayfly or
slow as a sermon. Either way,
you'll finally cross it.

Night Shuts In

The night nurse scares my veins apart.
Under the staircase the games are in gear.
The curtains exhale as I creep down the hall.
The floorboards complain of side effects.
The shape appears. The trial begins.
Under the blankets I cover my tracks.

Frank William Finney was born and raised in Massachusetts and spent many a summer in Maine. He moved to Thailand in 1995, where he taught literature at Thammasat University until the pandemic set in in 2020. He is the author of *The Dissolution of the Sparkling Bridge*, and *Songs of Insomnia* (published in Thailand by Suksit Siam). His poems have appeared in many literary journals, small press magazines, and anthologies since the 1980s including *Green Mountains Review, Orbis Quarterly International Journal, The Plentitudes, Slipstream Magazine, Positively Poetry: An Anthology of Little Press Poets, 1970-1995,* among others. A diploma prize winner in the 1997 Scottish International Poetry Competition, his poem "He Was Different" was selected by UA Fanthorpe for her "best hundred" out of 1,700 entries and subsequently chosen for a runner-up prize in the Staple Open Poetry Competition 1996-97 (UK).

www.ingramcontent.com/pod-product-compliance
Lightning Source LLC
LaVergne TN
LVHW041524070426
835507LV00012B/1807